75

- a number

- a passage

- a present

by

Audrey Ward

Illustrations by Olivia Ducharme

RoseDog Books

PITTSBURGH, PENNSYLVANIA 15238

RoseDog Books
585 Alpha Drive, Suite 103
Pittsburgh, PA 15238
Visit our website at *www.rosedogbookstore.com*

ISBN: 978-1-63661-016-0
eISBN: 978-1-63661-075-7

for

Tamara & Dan, Julie & Tom, Sam & Layla

yours are the nests where I love to be

for

Lauren Elisabeth
William Thomas
Olivia Sydney
Yasmin Natalie
Roselie Indiana
Zain Preston

wherever I wander, you are with me

75

- a number

- a passage

- a present

by

Audrey Ward

Illustrations by Olivia Ducharme

And I think to myself, I'll remember
this early dark and the rain, standing
before the toile-draped window, water
streaking the glass and dripping
from the low, curled iron, leaves
of wisteria vines, gold and green,
trembling in the November wind
that ruffles through Cour Damoye

I'll recall Olivier, the coffee man
who calls *bonjour* as he brews his exotic,
dark grinds in a small industrial shop
across the cobblestones.
And of course I can't forget how one
leans full-bodied into the great iron gate
opening it at midnight, coming home
from salsa-dancing, eating a hot dog.

I'll remember every moment in its own way
and for its own reason or for no reason
at all. I'll remember that on this Parisian lane
I was young one more time

Anchor

"...doing at 75 what I failed to do at 25," was my answer to questions about imminent retirement. My intention was carefree travel wherever the road seemed right, ending with two months in Paris; six weeks on the Cour Damoye, Bastille, and two weeks on the Quai D'Anjou, Île Saint-Louis.

Oh, there were friends along the way in Austria; meeting a colleague from Maine in Ireland. But after the first two weeks with grandchildren Olivia, 15, and Will, 17, as traveling companions, I would be on my own. I had no idea how daunting that would be.

Here are the jottings of doing what many said they envied. Here, also, are bits of life-review stories—from my Deep South childhood among Appalachian people to the elite neighborhoods of Europe and California—that were tagged by the places and people I encountered.

Hope anchors the future in all that we trust from the past. This was my song and assurance.

Besides, "I know how," I soothed myself by saying this when impish questions stacked up high as a rickety beaver's dam over a mountain stream.

I know how.

Don't Believe Everything You Think

So far, I haven't seen anything written about absurd prices in California real estate—buying or renting—that suggests one toss it all aside; put your belongings in storage and head to Paris. Or Vienna, or Prague. Maybe the South of France, near beaches you have known? Or even Italy. Leave.

Traveling has been a theme of my life. The memoir, *Hidden Biscuits*, witnesses to this.

Therefore, I only shrugged when I failed to find a replacement for the apartment I'd been listed to occupy for over 10 years which was now nearly tripled in price and without parking. Then I started packing.

But what I didn't possess was current intelligence about traveling with two teens. Will and Olivia, delightful human beings while visiting my house in the Napa Valley or when I was overseeing their household—including a younger sister, Roselie, eight—when parents were away.

They insisted my name for them during this trip would be *Pickles*. I failed to ask, "Is this a prediction?"

Other mysteries would quickly accrue: changing course in a set travel schedule. Trashing the train idea and flying, or that bus, FlixBus?

Even delightful human beings become agitated when there is no wifi (often), the temperature soars above anyone's comfort zone, and the train has nothing on board to eat except, say, sandwiches in cellophane that look at least a week old.

There was so much I did not know.

three

Pillows

Our hotel in Zurich, first night of arrival, included a Pillow Menu: True Story. Never before and never since have I experienced this display of luxury, but I like it.

After an 11-hour flight, one looks forward to resting one's weary head; now we could choose exactly how to do that in level of fluff as well as shape.

Out the door and across the street in the still-light summer evening was the silvery blue Zurichsee. We stroll along in balmy air, swans floating evenly with our stride. Occasionally we stop to take in the mountains beyond the city; the old trolleys' crisscrossing tracks up ahead as they discharge and pick up passengers going home for the night.

Will has lugged our bags into place, proving the weights he's been lifting at home were not in vain. And now Olivia snaps photos of our companions on the water side.

It's all, together, rather like a lullaby especially since we know our pillow menu will take us the rest of the way to heavenly places.

four

Pink

While Will finds a way to drape his lanky form wherever he sits, stands, leans or ambles, Olivia places her pink sneaker toes in odd poses then photographs them. They each have talents.

We could create one whole album of pink Vans pictures. Meeting a swan's bill while draped over the cement rim of the Zurichsee *snap*; pink toe rising in the air—perpendicular—to the hotel couch *snap*; poised up ahead in a pedal boat, *snap*.

It's reminiscent of her infant habit of propping a tiny foot—clad in its sock—on her high chair tray at the end of the meal. She was about six months old when this began: a hilarious-baby-trick of sucking her toes as a kind of delectable desert. Sometimes mashed squash or remnants of spinach were still in her mouth, of course, but no matter.

And now I adore this daily ritual, too. Plus, there's no cleaning job as a result.

Audrey Ward

Pedaling

There they go, the Pickles, out across the waters of the Zurichsee in their pedal boat. Such a sight all these years after their mother, Julie, and their Uncle Sam did the same at Renecros Beach in Bandol, France.

That time, it was in a small crescent-shaped inlet of the Mediterranean; this body of water in Switzerland is enormous. They're already tiny dots out there.

Was that the day Julie's delicate stomach revolted at the motion of the boat? I think so. You can guess what happened next. Yes. As I recall, it was a lunch of spaghetti. Colorful, I do remember that.

I have mercifully forgotten many details of my children's childhood escapades. Like what did the once-nice man say—no doubt in rapid, horrified French—when we checked the boat back in to the rental place? Or did we just leave it and run?

I did learn at my offsprings' very early ages that smiling big and getting as far away as I could before waving goodbye was sometimes the right thing to do when picking them up from daycare.

For me, now, it's enough to see Will and Olivia reenacting their mother's and uncle's tableau out on the water in a scene that will always make me smile.

Waze

Trips may be planned in advance but then they develop in their own snail trail of unfolding off-roads and side streets, railroad stations and airports, walkways or hidden passages.

The memory of a coffee shop may become immortalized as the one in Assisi where a morning espresso stop added a custard-filled croissant not of this world but descended from above.

Or so long ago at the train station in Pisa, where we were delayed, and as we waited there appeared a cup of hot chocolate no one has forgotten: an elixir unequaled ever since.

Tonight, Zurich's *bierstube*, Zeughauskeller, entertains with no opening act in its 15th century building. We sit at long tables where voices from all over the world topple over each other and great cold steins of brew are served.

Olivia rather favors her taste of *beir*. Will, not so much, but the sausages, mustard, and solid Swiss fare tell us exactly where we are.

Always, conversations that request directions come in at least two languages, one you speak; one you do not. And yet the nature of the person giving the instructions is so earnest that their kindness comes through.

Small details combine for one large adventure counted among our souvenirs. Even the lovely lady—really she was—whose market basket became caught in rolling over my foot.

"It was light," I said, "don't worry."

"Oh," she responded, in her heavy accent, "but I do."

Friends

First, it was Margit who saved us with an apartment in Linz, Austria. Then, her friends who have become my friends along the way, Christine and Herbert, rescued us by Herbert's taking the teenagers on a fling into the Austrian countryside, lake included.

A major reason I wanted to introduce Olivia and Will to Austria were the salt mines across the primordial lake in Halstatt. But, as life would have it, the day we were to go there, the winds were too strong to cross the lake. The ferry—a small boat with one conductor and space for about six people—would not be running.

Herbert and Christine know what 15 and 17 mean in terms that few may understand: they have had three such creatures pass through their home. And, Christine cooks to please the taste buds of every human alive; the growing boy among us was especially pleased.

Herbert fetched the Pickles—though he'd only seen their pictures—from a street fair in Linz by using the "safe word," *Audrey.* We arranged via cell phone for him to find them at a particular corner: very James Bond.

That began an afternoon of sightseeing and then swimming in local waters. He knew a lake where other teens were hanging out around a rubber-tire-contraption that hurls one into the lake for a wild ride.

Sundown returned them exhausted and starving to Leonding, the Hallers' quiet village and their home's garden of paths through roses, where Christine's cuisine soothed us into evening.

Never have I treasured my friends more.

Wifi

Can we fix it? My pal—a New York attorney—would ask her assistant when they crashed into a road block. The answer is, of course: not always.

FlixBus is the fastest way to Prague from Linz, Austria: four hours, nonstop, while the train meanders through back gardens for six hours before reaching her destination. We were already exhausted by trashed, weary train travel.

So, there we were, first in line early Monday morning at the FlixBus stop. Our only cover was a misty veil of Austrian drizzle.

Without a reservation, however, you have no priority. Turns out you must do everything by websites even when you don't have wifi. Yep. That's a rule.

It's an *unwritten* rule, but aren't most of them? In Southern France when I bought a week-long wifi package from a local dealer, I had to have wifi in order to set it up. Right.

While a long queue of people with their reservations firmly in hand boarded the cozy autobus, we stood wondering if we would make the list in what had now become a deluge. Herbert was on alert, ready to speed to our rescue if we didn't finally land inside.

This was the day I discovered my smart new luggage was not waterproof. We already knew we weren't.

As we were conducted through the Austrian countryside toward the Czech Republic, I was grateful for wearing clothes built for hiking that dry as they go.

          Audrey Ward

nine

Stop

As long as we were speeding through Prague—luxuriating in the city of castles, rivers to cross and back alleys to explore—there was only time to eat, sleep and go again.

But I knew we needed to stop. Figure out what's next, where, how?

We crossed the Charles Bridge in an ancient convertible whose driver recognized where we must go: he took us a hidden way to a dead-end street where there is a memorial for John Lennon. Louche young people whispered and smoked; drew on the graffiti-walls that protected someone's private garden.

Olivia and Will leaned against the reds, blues and greens, yellows blended to gold, words stretched into symbols and rolled into meanings known only to the artists. I snapped their picture beneath an arch of blue paint "SAVE THE HUMANS."

Finally, while racing back to Vienna by rail, there was time to revel in wifi, and exhale. The next two days—with our hosts Judit and Eduardo as our guides—would be our last time-out kind of luxury. After that, an exact schedule was required for imagining the Pickles' final week of vacation.

And so, Will, Olivia, and I dreamed up the rest of the time until August first. Here's how we decided it would go: flying from Vienna to Zurich with a private car waiting to take us up into the Alps.

What we couldn't yet see was that this would trip us into terrain with a mile-down drop to a village in the valley, while at the top we watched a hang glider waft into air suffused pink from setting sun. All this, as we dawdled at our table on the terrace after dinner.

It was well worth being still long enough to figure it out.

Friends II

The train to Vienna from Prague, I knew by now, would only be tolerable if it had decent seating and *wifi*: Business Class, no other option.

Judit and Eduardo, linguists extraordinaire, live in Vienna after years of her interpreting French and Hungarian for the United Nations and his being part of a number of international organizations. This pair is the definition of amazing grace as far as I'm concerned.

Eduardo met the train with his usual brio and guided Olivia, William, and me onto a grand city bus—parked at the curb out front—as if he were directing a parade. Then we were on to the hotel just steps away from their apartment. This part of the city cools her streets with leafy majesty, yet is on a direct route to the center.

I didn't prepare the young ones for our walk, later, to the Austrian country café where we were to have dinner. Probably I forgot about Judit's difficulty until we were on our way. I usually do: because of a bout with Polio as a child, her one leg is considerably shorter than the other.

And so, we progressed slowly. If one isn't used to it, the pace may even seem painfully slow. They were in awe of her patience with herself and of Eduardo's matter-of-fact role as helper.

After a while, we pointed the way, and the young ones headed off to reserve a place for us at the ancient eating establishment.

Will remembers the apricot dumplings there. They both remember Judit's lesson for them in being a graceful life.

 Audrey Ward

Soup

Never have I ever duplicated the lentil spinach soup from the Hundertwasser Museum Café in Vienna: one of my goals in life. This little vegetarian dining area in the courtyard beckoned Judit and me on a warm summer afternoon, late as it was for lunch.

We were greeted by a fragrant mélange, thick enough to satisfy the soul as well as the appetite and tasty with herbs as yet unidentified. Spinach, too, introduced so seamlessly, one hardly noticed it at all.

Perhaps it was the place that made it so entirely delicious. We were wandering in the artist's house of dark wood with its splashes of brilliant blue, green, yellow, and white; sloped floors, a twisting staircase; a hallway terrarium and an installation of black and white tiles surprising yet satisfying in their setting. The senses are unshackled, ready to receive.

Lentils are plentiful in Europe, so I tried to reconstruct the soup at my place in Bandol and several times in Paris to no avail.

If you have such a recipe, send it to me. Please.

Oblivious

Airplanes carry
crowds of people,
never meeting
in another place
or time; not
introduced now, either.
Suspended in space,
row after row
of disconnected
strangers
share their lives,
their experience;
share their fate,
for these few hours:
oblivious of
the outcome.
Simply gliding,
silent, through
an inky blue sky
above the clouds
without questions.

Audrey Ward

Home

The train—resembling a toy—took me and the young ones to the top of Europe the morning after we arrived at our airy perch in the Swiss Alps. Red, square cars hooked together in a row trailing up to the Jungfraujoch. It is the world's steepest railway.

A stop midway at Kleine Schedegg intersected a sunshine-colored carrier coming from Wengen. They have the merry look of playing with us and each other, spilling out hikers with backpacks, walking sticks, and many-zippered vests above shorts, then slurping up some more.

Here's where I found an old leather strap with a cow bell attached. I love this haunting sound remembered from watching goats or cows wend their way through mountain passages in France, Spain, Italy, Austria, and now, Switzerland.

Every spring when storms are past, the cows are led up to high pastures to feast on the plentiful, bright grass. Then in September, villages have a day of celebration when the cows come home, back to the barns that often share a common wall with the house of their farm family.

Flower garlands adorn the necks of the parading animals, bands play; beer and sausages are plentiful for the villager's celebrational feast. That's one festival I've always hoped to attend.

But then that goes with the theme of my reality: always searching for home. This condition is no doubt a result of growing up in an 18-foot trailer house as we bumped along from one backwoods post to another in the Deep South.

And yet, look at this: what a wonderful life along the way, I say.

fourteen

High

The Lauterbrunnen Valley stretches so far away—11,000 feet—that the tiny towns nestled there are barely visible.

After Will and Olivia explore the glacier, we descend by way of Wengen, a village of treasured memories in my reveries of traveling with their mother, Julie, and her brother, Sam.

They were 12 and 14 at the time we arrived at the Wengen train station in the middle of a torrential rainstorm. Since there are no cars in the village, we were taken to our tiny *auberge* in the back of a golf cart protected from the downpour by inadequate umbrellas. Arriving, however, we found down comforters on each bed to cozy our cold, wet selves, with chocolates on the bedside table. *Heaven.*

Nothing was visible outside our windows on that late afternoon, but when we pulled back the heavy velvet drapes the next morning, the Jungraujoch was there in brilliant sunshine before us. Speechless awe was all we could muster.

But now, the day is balmy with a fragrance near spring in the air even in late summer. We transfer to a *teleferique* from the train to go over the mountain to Grindelwald.

Pausing at the summit in Mürren, Olivia rides a kid's iron toy horse in a playground as we await a second, smaller car down. Just beyond her, cows graze amidst brilliant blue wild flowers before the terrain descends a mile to a misty village in the valley.

Only one more day and then it's back to Zurich. Their home-going is way too close.

 Audrey Ward

fifteen

Loss

Loss can propel one's lurch into a strong sense of feeling *old*. Not necessarily losing a person—no—but something as ordinary as a vest.

Mind you, it was a favorite: the vest with grosgrain ribbon securing her buttons; pockets, two at hip level that could be reached in front, but then slipped into from the side as well.

It was that day I journeyed from the Zurich airport—after watching the tops of two beloved blond heads disappear down the moving stairway—then finding the bus to Interlaken. After that, connecting to the train for Wengen where I had reservations for a few days before continuing into Italy, destined for Lake Como.

Discouraged, hot, exhausted, I settled into the last lap of the journey back up the mountain. Hurriedly alighting at the quick stop in Wengen, it was not until I walked into the serene Alpine lodge that I suddenly realized my vest was still on the train.

I wept.

Oh sure, it was only one small garment, but that tiny personal symbol became the occasion for pouring forth my grief: the larger partings in career, separation from family, farewells, and *what now?* A sensation of being old, useless, beyond hope, overwhelmed me.

It became a magical vest with great powers, evoking years full of regrets. All of it accumulated in a rush as I sat looking over the unspeakable beauty of a window box spilling tiny golden daisies into a vast mountainous terrain.

And through the emotional veil and the visual drama came the occasional call of the train's whistle as it continued to its destination.

That evening, there was a white wine—I always drink red—at that inn whose name I recorded: Swiss, of course, *Fendant Léon*. If

Audrey Ward

given an opportunity, do not miss an opportunity for a glass of this elixir.

Perhaps the pale, lovely wine possesses magic, too, because that night *Fendant Léon* soothed my ragged soul.

sixteen

Forgot

I Forgot   (In the manner of Eileen Tabios' *Amnesia*)

I forgot that on my birthday, I must write a letter, an ode one might say,
    to myself.
I forgot this is vital, for time meanders, missing notes, losing vests,
    and crying for milk not even spilt.
I forgot that the way of travel is long, tedious and distracting.
I forgot that the loves of my life pop up when I'm far away;
    their voices sing, a guitar sways, and longing surfaces like a
    taunt, a misplaced embrace, a first kiss. And a last.
I forgot that in the remembering there cannot be clinging or regret,
    only melodious balm for the soul.
I forgot that even loss is worth the loving. Every love leads to loss.
I forgot that here in Wengen, the village so high in the Alps no cars
    can reach, an early morning walk with Robert, holding
    hands, was full of delight: fresh bread left on a ledge by a win-
    dow, rock gardens in the mist.
I forgot that my life is much more about loving than losing.
I forgot that love is warmly recalled however the ending may come.
And I forgot that my birthday is worth a fine tribute, for wherever
    I am may well be a place of new birth.

        Audrey Ward

Connection

What I learned from my up-front stated "reason" for taking a five-month journey on my own turned out to be exactly the opposite.

In fact, I do need companions along the way. Going it alone as if it doesn't matter taught me that indeed it does.

Not because I don't like being alone; I do.

Not because I'm in dread of appearing single in restaurants; I'm not at all.

Not even because often two sets of eyes and ears are needed when you're in a strange place without language or familiar sign posts and have three trains to line up just to reach an overnight in Lucerne; then more trains, one of which will disconnect at a switch plus a bus and then a ferry to get to Bellagio on Lake Como. No, not even all that.

Rather, it's what Roger Angell wrote in his iconic piece for the New Yorker, titled, "This Old Man": *The second most surprising thing in my life was growing old; the first, by a mile, was the unceasing need for deep connection and intimacy.*

Yeah. That.

Parmesan

It was a pasta dish I ordered for lunch on the terrace of a little place in Bellagio overlooking Lake Como one steamy August day, that I will never forget. Something simple was my aim, since the fumes from ferries coming and going in the port made me feel nauseated; I thought this might settle me down.

The only ingredients were a light sauce—or only butter?—fettuccine, and parmesan, but the trick was how this was accomplished: the woman serving me rolled out a wooden tray on which rested an entire round of Parmesan. She dumped the hot saucy pasta into the indented center of the cheese and with two large spoons proceeded to toss it about while taking gouges out of the walls of the round and incorporating each piece into the pasta. Wow.

Never before nor since have I seen such a display of simple culinary perfection. Sensational in every possible way.

I doubt if anything could have settled my nausea to a slow rocking on that day, but no matter. I took most of it back to my delicious apartment at the top of the hill and enjoyed it later that night when the air had cooled and the moon illumined the water.

I ate—gazing out the giant casement windows of La Casa Rosa—savoring the creation of the dish just as I do now in remembering.

Majestic

My time in the apartment at La Casa ended, but I didn't want to leave the area. That was when I innocently rented a toxic apartment just outside Bellagio.

Fortunately, there was an 11th century chapel one block away. Simple, rebuilt, and restored; eloquent in her silence. She restored me, as well. I believe that small sacred space saved my life. Why not? Something certainly did.

The morning I finally got out of the space I had leased, my throat hurt so much I couldn't—*could not*—swallow. It was a very strange sensation since all I was trying to down was coffee and a croissant.

Later, a medical man told me that this is the first physical indication that one's body is shutting down: the throat closes. It was my physical response to a gas leak in the apartment.

Every moment I could steal away, I went to the chapel at the end of this dusty road with orange flowering vines of summer climbing along the walls of her houses. I remember the light inside this sanctuary as golden; simple wooden benches; majestic angels adorning candlesticks on the altar. A chapel dedicated to Mary.

The prayers were centered in a child. But while we pray for others, aren't we praying for ourselves as well? My hunch is that's what's going on in times of sacred exchange.

That old spiritual, "It's Me, It's Me Oh Lord, Standin' in the Need of Prayer," agrees that, *yes, it is*. Always.

Triumph

Extricating myself from that second apartment in Bellagio turned out to be its own saga. Easy enough, I thought, to take the ferry to the next village where the train would take me into *Milano Centrale*. And it was.

Enduring the grime of the Milano train station lasted only a few seconds as I rushed out to a taxi, directing the driver to the FlixBus station; which, it turns out, resembles a small third world country with no food or beverage services except for a few broken-down vending machines. I had about 10 hours to kill before the scheduled trip began at 9:00 that night.

My reasoning was that this FlixBus ride would take me through the night to Linz, Austria, and once there, I'd be back to Margit's place at a familiar bus stop, too. I was wrong.

Meantime, I bargained with a taxi driver at the bus terminal to take me somewhere that had food and beverage access. That's how I arrived at a 24-hour cafeteria that was an ideal place to loiter while reading *The New York Times International Edition*. Write a few lines. Have a cappuccino; repeat.

Here I encountered another of my savior-figures—there were many along the way—in the form of an American professor and his two young children. They dashed in to buy sandwiches for their trip to a nearby lake; I asked him where I could find a taxi stand in the area.

He directed me to a five-star hotel in walking distance. There I became acquainted with the kind, friendly bartender and lounged in the lobby, including a brief nap, before going back to the terminal at nine.

Rain arrived as the crowded bus moved through an Italian night into Austria at dawn. But the stop in Linz was in the industrial section where I had never been. The driver opened the luggage portal on the traffic side and plopped my bags onto the roadway in blinding rain. As I stood there trying to figure out how to get across, he sped away.

I finally spied a lighted local bus, stopped at the end of the line a short distance away; found my way to the train station, a taxi, and, drying myself off as I fell into bed, my last thought was: *Ha! I did it. And at 75, no less.* I did it.

Breakdown

Dickens' philosophy fits my exhaustion on a rainy Austrian day. His small volume tossed aside in this attic book shelf meets the sodden miles I've traveled in every vehicle known to human kind with a shrug for human effort.

My mulling over a lifespan of bearing children and raising men plus earning a living—while learning a way that strained to make a difference—points to a crossroads of dead ends right now. Is this true, I wonder, and where's the reality?

But Dickens splashes cold water in the face of my weary mood. Destiny is the interruption of happenstance, the ditch by the side of the road unseen until one's wagon wheel comes flying off and lands there, broken, never more to hum along the roadway headed for a destination.

Virtue, Charles reminds me, may not be its own reward or any recompense at all. And the ditch by the side of the road *is* the road.

Ireland

Here's what I did: simply on the suggestion that perhaps I'd like to meet a long-time friend who would be there that week, I took a flight from Vienna across the waters to the Emerald Isle.

Priscilla is a United Methodist colleague from Maine. Over four years' time, we worked together in New York on behalf of children who've been injured by predators. This kind of collaboration creates very special bonds.

After meeting in Dublin, we took a bus to Killarney and checked into a bed and breakfast full of history and surrounded by flowers.

My long walk in the late afternoon brought me to a meadow of grazing sheep out back of a deluxe country hotel. I adore sheep—friends in France called me *Petit Mouton* because of a certain resemblance—but what I most remember of that meadow is the misty light: breathtaking in its ethereal reality. It was as if the glow came from elsewhere, somewhere celestial.

Next day, on we traveled to the Dingle Peninsula, where we struggled our luggage up the hill from the bus stop. In the rain. Hoping we had found our cozy B & B at last, we asked the rosy-cheeked woman who answered the door,

"Are you Eileen?"

"The very one," she responded.

Her charm as a warm detail of this country was further enhanced by a tiny bouquet of sweet peas on our late afternoon tea tray; whenever these blossoms appear, so does my mother.

We have a ticket for music at St. James Church tonight. Rain is still falling, of course: how else is Ireland to continue being an Emerald Isle?

ɠɔ

She's coming into view slowly, but surely: Yes, Ireland, "the very one."

　　　Audrey Ward

Beloved

Ireland encourages minstrels of all kinds, shapes and sizes: in the bars, at the restaurant, or along an avenue.

A fine guitarist and his singing muse sold tickets to their concert at St. James Church, a clean, well-lighted, white interior of an old sanctuary now used as a venue space. I am convinced that music is God's language, so this works well for me.

But what most arrested my attention as we awaited the beginning of the double-troubadour's performance, was the framed message on the wall:

In memory of
Mary Mc Donell
beloved wife and devoted helper
of Rev. Charles Kingsley
for 8 years in Dingle.
She slept in Jesus 12 May 1878
in her 35th year.
Her life was love.
Her death, glory
and from that glory the echo of
her voice seems still to repeat
the message which on earth
was her delight,
"come to the Savior."
Mt 11:25

The music paled in my reverie of this Mary, a woman who was so adored that her memory is engraved on a wall. No one forgets her now, even those whom she never met: *Her life was love…*

Healing

Where words fail, music speaks.
– Hans Christian Anderson

Life itself continues apace whether I am present to be a witness or not. Reports of friends come to me day by day.

Wesla goes into Hospice. David has been struggling with his diagnosis for over a year. I have no way of knowing whether I will ever see either of them—and others—again. People I cherish every day.

David

When he was well, his music-adoration
quotient was the highest
of any other known human.
David could not leave a piece of music without the finish; if in the car,
for example, one had to pause while Beethoven's 3rd completed.
And so, when he moved in with the beautiful blue-eyed
pianist who had a Steinway instead of a television
in the den, no one was surprised.

Now, in his days of distress, I can imagine
his brow smooth as the music moves in
and rolls through his failing body: melodious
compositions are still his companions and finest
medicine. Their harmony always heals him.

And here, so far away, I remind myself that sometimes we are healed into life; sometimes we are healed into death: there is always healing. Always.

twenty-five

Voice

Sundays, all European cities tag team church bells begun in one tower to echo in another across town, heralding the hour that gathers in the faithful. A signal that God's basket full of hopefuls are stopping the week to get off.

In Linz, Austria, needing to find a way to fill the day after my traveling companions had departed, I attended the protestant service downtown. Sure, it would be in German, but the cadence of voices in reading scripture; the music played and sung, still soothes my soul after so many years of conditioning.

To my surprise—and pleasure—there was a pair of hounds who graced the side aisle with their distinguished master. They quietly participated simply through their presence: *All Creatures of Our God and King*.

Not until I arrived in Paris did my Sundays become undiluted pleasure: the American Cathedral satisfied every cell of my brain, body, and soul.

Dean Lucinda Laird is an oral tradition preacher. Unimaginable that I would land in a place where, whenever she stood to speak, I felt a connection to all 33 years of doing exactly this. No notes, just stand and deliver.

I could appreciate in her what I couldn't see in myself. When we had lunch one day, she confessed the same reluctance to forsake the big words and references to elaborate sources that I have. Questions pop up, "Should I make an effort to seem…more scholarly… what?"

But then one's own voice may be lost in the litter of importance writ large. A message that arrives in simple terms is far more portable; the hearer can take it home. And, perhaps, take it to heart as the days go by.

Lucinda Laird will always be salve for my preacher's soul.

Velcro

Entry into Paris from the airport invariably reflects that day in 1976 when Bob Ward, my husband of a few weeks, drove in by way of circling the Arc d'Triumph and up the Grand Boulevard. He was proud of giving me this gift of awe at first sight and so am I, always.

Ever since, of course, no matter how I arrive, it is this image that snaps onto it, quickly transforming the ordinary early morning taxi or train ride through a vision of the past.

The Marais Hotel de JoBo, has some kind of magical power, too. Rooms are tiny at the de JoBo but every inch is covered in wallpaper or fabric, reminiscent of Old Paris: the way she nudged the rest of the world to notice elegance and grandeur. It feels like home.

I stopped there only one night in order to leave my winter bag to be stashed at my apartment for later arrival in October. But when I needed to crash for a couple of nights in transition at another point, the de JoBo was my choice. She feels like shelter, nestled close by a leafy square with four cafés facing off day into night.

Rodin's house possesses the sway to transport a casual visitor into a resident as well. Musée Rodin is found a few blocks before the end of bus line #69. After a writing, nomadic morning and lunch for as long as one chooses to linger in his garden cafe, walk back to the Musée D'Orsay on the Seine. There's always something going on along her steps.

Rest there before the long stroll home. Or, cross over to the right bank and wait for the bus while gazing into the rhythms and colors of the river.

And as you pause, savor the twords of W.S. Merwin: *What you come to remember becomes yourself.*

Delicious

What is it about a smart person serving up a dollop of wit along with his informed talk that is so much fun? Nothing obsequious, no need to fawn or wallow in faux generalities fluffed for the occasion with ribbons or bows.

One exhales on sight and that pleasure doesn't diminish even through health descriptions that edge on deep concerns.

John Sam and I are both mired in language study: he, working on German since he and his husband moved to a small village near the Dutch-German border. And my French is definitely—always—under construction.

The two of us are in deep conversation as we stroll, whether along the Loire or headed into the village for dinner. Moving through a hallway as we talk, or in and out of doorways, here, means vaulted rooms of chateaux, across vast lawns bordered in woods; low rock walls defining a village that we're exploring along the river.

Too soon, luggage is waiting by the breakfast room door. My throat tightens with good-byes. John Sam waves to me as I head into the train station.

We never know if there will be another hello. Yet learning to say each word well—*hello* and *goodbye*—secures the life lesson we're required to learn. *Farewell*, said with grace, will smooth the entry for the next, *It's you!*

That's why I call it, *Delicious*. Yes. It is.

 Audrey Ward

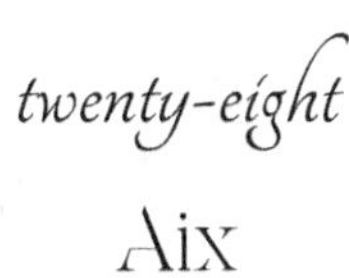

twenty-eight

Aix

Train travel in the countries I visited—Austria, France, Ireland, Italy, Switzerland, Czech Republic—is anything but intuitive for this American. Can't you just buy a ticket on the *chemin de fer* and go any direction? No.

Instead one may have to go back to Paris and leave from a different station for a new destination. The same is true with British trains; London is the hub. It can be both complicated and frustrating enough to sit. Stay.

So at first, that's what I did: when I could neither rent a car (they were out) nor go to Aix-en-Provence from Orléans, I called the de JoBo (for Josephine/Bonaparte) in Paris and reserved the only room they had left for the next couple of days to give me time to figure it out. There was a ticketing office for the train just a block away, and I was able to find an accommodating agent to work with me.

Aix-en-Provence swarms with summertime visitors as well as students, year 'round. I remember it with great pleasure from when we lived about an hour away in 1980. One shop in particular always provided the perfect little thing: wide ribbons (there was a basket full of them) as a new belt. Or a short, loose-weave white dress, the kind that demands response when one shows up in it.

Favorite chic little shops seem to have disappeared, however, with the influx of tours, both by bus and by ship. Places once elegant like Venice or Aix have lost their particularity through trinket and t-shirt stands.

Across the street from the magnificent fountain at the Aix roundabout is what? An Apple store. Trust me, you can't miss it.

I spent a lot of time looking out over the square from the perch on my balcony. Late at night or early morning when the streets were being washed clean for the day, I covered the town on foot.

Finally, I was perfectly happy to board the TGV there—*Train à Grande Vitesse,* "high speed train"—for rapid delivery to Marseille transferring to a local that would leave me in Bandol for two weeks.

Venasque

A walled, medieval town at the foot of Mont Ventoux was a turning point for our family: here, Bob and I decided one morning in early spring when cherry trees bloomed on the hills all around, that some-day we would return and live in Provence. And we did.

And so, at the end of my sojourn in Aix, I rented a car to visit this beloved village near Avignon.

The car was reserved at the train station outside town. That's where my adventure on the RN7 up into the wilds of Provence began. Detours in reaching the *autoroute* were my first hurdles, but even in the madness of "detours" becoming dead ends, after I finally arrived on the highway, I could see that an exit was going to prove difficult as well: **Rousillon** fills that in.

But the reward for the complexity of the trip was the definite *Yes* to Venasque. So small is this place, there is no room for tour buses to park. A bonus. When I saw that villages such as Gorde, which I intended to visit, had enormous parking lots for tour buses, I learned to skip them.

Not that I don't like tourists since I am one, but the dripping ice cream cones, okay, *crème glacée*, and overheard bits of conver-sation like, "…this is just like Italy…" were too much to bear in large doses.

The *auberge* where Bob and I stayed so long ago was not avail-able for guests anymore, so I had booked a bed and breakfast in the valley just below Venasque where I could look up into her grace as I wrote or rested midst the grape vines near the pool. That was, of course, after I purchased a warm baguette at the *boulangerie* and a fat slice of country paté in the one-aisle *epicerie*.

Then, too, I lingered at the church whose foundation for the baptistry dates to the 8th century. Since this sanctuary is in daily consecrated use, one can feel the prayers in her warmth along with catching a whiff of roses from local gardens on her altar.

We were so right, I confirmed, in deciding for our future based on this hallowed village.

thirty

Roussillon

To Roussillon

Here, I learned to sail roundabouts;
maintain steely patience
sur le Route A7—Toutes Directions—
kept my head
when the two cars in front of me
began to back up
in the A7 toll booth
and I did not freak out
when the toll booth arm
came down across my rental car.

The rest stop was a capital idea
to regroup, recoup my senses
and head *Direction* Cavaillon:
the nearest town off this
highway riddle with a clearly defined
ramp to leave, I imagined (almost true).
Anyhow, it worked. Now,
with a French bath tub filled to the brim,
                            a code for my well-being;
I need nothing more.

Dictation

Nothing matters as much as the child within us. This little one dictates according to the life she lived back when—unchartered—she was directed according to her parent's intentions.

My undiluted pleasure in new places owes itself to those roads in the South, sometimes stretching out to San Francisco to see Aunt Dorie and Uncle Al, my father's siblings. And at least every decade or so, our going to Western Canada to visit Aunt Lucia and her large brood of beautiful, bright offspring.

But it was Calvert School in Baltimore, through their correspondence school, that taught me to love learning: a gift of pure gold. For me, it means I'm always a student, constantly studying.

When given a chance to spend a summer at Oxford, Christ Church, I hopped right on it. Challenging as a couple of the classes were, I loved every minute.

That child in me has a well-developed curiosity from those years of constant travel, learning from the landscape, the people and their culture plus school books as we went along the back roads and byways. When asked for advice on occasion, this is all I offer: *Stay Curious.*

Then, perhaps I add this: if you're a parent, be aware of what is being dictated to your children. Whatever a child learns from that transcription lasts an entire lifetime.

La plage

Watching Julie and Sam play in the surf just steps away while Bob and I enjoyed a three course *déjeuner* was just one of the pleasures of Renecros, a sheltered, crescent-shaped beach on the Mediterranean in Bandol.

It might have been soup and salad or a savory stew, whatever the special of the day, but the important part was that our lunch was served with a liter of wine—usually rosé—and we could take a nap as sea breezes cooled us afterward. What sensory loveliness.

From about April, on, until we left in July (so we could miss the rest of Europe when they flooded into Provence) we spent two or three days a week at Renecros. And so, when I found a studio apartment about a block away that was right on the water, I booked it for the last two weeks of September.

My only disappointment—besides that it is no longer a topless beach as it was when we lived nearby—was being there without anyone from the family joining me.

Not a single time I walked by or sat on the sand watching the stunning blues of sky and sea, though, did they fail to show up in my reveries.

thirty-three

Seeing

What I wrote in my journal that exquisite blue and gold day at the beach town on the French Mediterranean, was, "Well, at least I'm not in jail. I came close to beating up a Frenchman, father of four."

We were all enjoying the sunshine at the fountain café in this town square I so love, with towering palm trees and a breeze straight out of heaven, on a terrace overlooking the sea. The two younger children of the family just in front and to the side of me were playing back and forth, a beautiful blonde girl with bouncing curls and a sunny little boy, laughing and then, of course, getting into a bit of a fracas.

Not loud or terrible, just childish bantering of slight disagreement, when their handsome father reached out and pulled their hair so hard it sickened me. The girl, about five, was instantly silent, stoic, and moved out of reach; the boy, younger, not as prepared for his father's casual cruelty spilled tears as he quietly murmured his pain.

The father stood—mother ignored the whole thing—and walked over to the bar next door for a pack of cigarettes. Suddenly, his profile looked vile to me; his expensive clothes no longer adorning.

And some day, I thought to myself, he will say of his younger son, "He's never amounted to much." The scene shook me, including the mother's disregard for her grieving children, not even offering comfort to the boy who leaned against her, imploring.

By the girl's reaction, it seems that this was not her first experience with her parent's aggression. She knew not to seek her mother's help.

Seeds of violence are planted in the body; pain comes to maturity as a habit of the soul.

Care

No matter where I am, I remember the children whom I've served for over 30 years as pastor. Not only in the churches where I was appointed, of course, but in the communities around them.

It started with a child named Jeremiah. Wherever on Earth I may roam, he never leaves me: his tousled blond hair and his dazzling smile as he looked into the camera that day are always with me. That photo is all I knew of him. I never saw Jeremiah alive, only his small white casket.

He was brutally, slowly murdered over a nine-month period by his mother's boyfriend, the man who supplied her with drugs. His final blow came when the child was three years old.

From then, on, I was determined that not only this congregation but every one I served—as well as the larger United Methodist denomination—would become aware of their children's needs. We began an educational program for his impoverished county through a rugged little effort called *HomePeace…because world peace begins at home.*

Ultimately, I left the church for two years to work for their District Attorney as we established the Children's Council. The ultimate gift—besides free educational programs for both parents and children—was a major state grant for families and children. All in the name of a beautiful little boy who loved life but was taken from it too soon.

For Jeremiah, I notice children in my environment; I always follow them with my heart.

Ratatouille

My first go-to dish that I prepare when I have my own kitchen in Europe is *ratatouille*, perhaps as an homage to our sojourn in Provence. We lived on vegetables—*courgette, aubergine, ail, tomate*—and baguette for a couple of months when the French bank we trusted with our account played with our money wired from the States on the international exchange instead of turning it over to us when it arrived.

Finally, our neighbor whom we picked up along our country route after her little car ran out of gas, took us to meet her husband at his bank in La Ciotat. He was head of the second largest ship building company in France. When he introduced us to his banker, amazingly, our funds never took more than 24 hours to appear.

It is who one knows wherever it may be, that's true, but it's always the *ratatouille* that comforts me.

Really

She was surprised, my landlord from Bandol, that this silver haired woman was traveling alone. The genteel owner of my resting place along the Mediterranean for two weeks, carefully navigating her BMW through the narrow passages, raised her eyebrows.

And after this, Paris for two months? *Vraiment?*

She was curious. How did I find this place in Paris?

An ad in the back of a friend's Stanford Alumni magazine.

And what was my inspiration to make such a trip?

75. *Soixante-quinze.*

Vraiment? Really.

Eliane

Bandol brought a flood of memories as I rode the bus to Sanary sur Mer on market day and cooked soup or *ratatouille* in my miniscule kitchen like Eliane would have done.

Here's how we met: Julie and Sam had lessons from their teachers in California to do in the morning, but they went to the local one-room country school of only 12 children—ages five through 12—in the afternoon for playmates and access to language. We took the kids their ages to the beach for a picnic one Wednesday—there was class on Saturday morning instead—and later when we drove her two sons home, Eliane invited us in for an *aperitif*.

That began my captivating friendship with a woman who was proud to be a Provençal Peasant. Hands rough as a construction worker told of her hard life, but as she taught me how to cook local dishes in her sod-floored kitchen, she expressed her soft, warm generosity.

Eliane was often hired to prepare elegant meals for homes of diplomats and people with *residence secondaire* who came from Marseille or Paris. Her own house, however, was a Provençal *mas* with farm animals sharing part of it. As we cooked—*ratatouille, anchoiade, aioli, île flotante*—a donkey might stick his head through the beads hung across the kitchen doorway with his loud cheerful greeting.

While I was again here in Bandol, I rented a car to find their dusty road. There it was, her husband Roland's name on the mailbox but with a different female name alongside.

My memory returned of Eliane's describing physical complications the last time I saw her; I now understood they ominously pre-

dicted a shadowed ending too soon. I searched for her in the church-
yard of Sainte Anne, too, but only the rich are buried there.

It was she who returned me to the treasured Appalachian people
of my childhood described in *Hidden Biscuits*. Though we had titled, important friends when we lived in Provence it is Eliane who
holds the most prominent place in my heart.

thirty-eight

Entry

That was the first day of October when the lovely woman who had met me at the train in Bandol on September 15 came to her apartment along the *bord du mer* to take me back to the station.

Her summer rental is a large studio looking directly into the waters of the Mediterranean. From this perch, I saw one lone fisherman putter out before dawn to work his nets and traps every morning except today, Sunday. *Dimanche*, his sabbath rest.

First destination was Toulon, where the TGV—*le train plus vite*—took me quickly (about three hours) to Paris. The whole Journey of 75 had been awaiting this particular trip.

At August's end, I had zoomed through the City of Light, stopping only one night at the Hotel JoBo. There, Teresa's service person for the apartment in Cour Damoye, Daud, had picked up my winter suitcase to keep for my October arrival.

So many helping hands: Every kilometer of the journey people I trusted—some, complete strangers—showed up to knit together my pieces so that I could arrive whole.

Forevermore, I decided, as I sat at the local wood floored café a few blocks from my Paris home, savoring their special for the day—beef bourguignon—and quaffing a nice quantity of house red, the first day of October will be, *The Entry into Paris, 75.*

And I laughed out loud.

Audrey Ward

Security

My tentacles for what isn't my safety zone were sensitized by a rambling childhood.

Walking into the unfamiliar will do that for you: Quick! Who's here? What's the atmosphere telling me?

From a small town post office to a big time church vestibule, it's a rapid read. One learns to observe signals and gauge accordingly. And no one, I'll wager, more than I when it comes to the experience of sanctuaries.

Online, my first day in Paris, I checked out a prominent American church along the Seine. Their midweek program sounded, well, probably conservative, but c'mon Audrey, be a sport.

So on what I remembered as the appointed evening I found my way to the church, walking many blocks; arriving early. But not *that* early: there was no one else there.

The kind watchman let me come into the entryway of the sanctuary to read the notice board. A feeling overcame me there, as if my entire body had been attacked by buzzing angry insects.

Of course, it was nothing of the sort, but only my antennae's clear, distinct signal: this is *not* the place for you.

Whew. I was glad I misremembered the day and did not spend a Sunday on this address. Later, I did attend a community Thanksgiving service and understood more clearly what an ill fit it would have been.

The experience served to remind me yet again: *The Body Knows.*

forty

Francis

By far my most beloved Sunday at the Cathedral—The American Cathedral of Paris—was the celebration of St. Francis; the Blessing of the Animals. Every size of dog, carriers full of cats, a very large bunny, plus stuffed animals to represent those at home or as substitute, came through the massive carved doors, gathering in the ancient stone sanctuary to worship.

Just like the rest of us.

This shelter felt hallowed as few have in my years—lifetime—of church going: all God's creatures, together.

A couple of dogs had a conversation. Yes, the nervous little one yipping, yipping, yipping—and no one apparently able to comfort—until the deep voice in the bark of authority silenced the complaint. I so-wished I knew what the Big Guy said.

An odd result of this particular Sunday was that ever-after, I would see the man who brought the giant bunny, carrying him in his arms up the aisle to be blessed; or the boy whose sweet German Short-Haired Pointer was so perfectly mannered and quiet; the woman pulling a wagon with the carrier of what must have been a Maine Coon cat, so grand an animal was he: each person who had brought an animal that day appeared somewhat altered after that.

Each one more endearingly human, somehow.

forty-one

Path

Psalm 111
(translated by Stephen Mitchell)

All beings perform his covenant and act out his primal law:
that whatever we reap, we have sown and what we give, we
receive.
To know this is the beginning of wisdom, to live it is the path
of true life.

Sometimes it takes a lot longer than we imagined to live this out, the giving and receiving. While I want it as a boomerang effect, it works more like a 12- or even 20-year turnaround.

In the weariness of waiting, I writhe and contort; flipping about caused by my faithlessness in life. Anxiety, after all, isn't proof of serious purpose or wisdom.

And then, just when I least expect it, the Psalmist's phrases come to me in the night, as I'm falling asleep in the soft golden covers of the place on Cour Damoye, Paris.

Fragile

There's fragility in both perceived and actual aging. Missing a last step and twisting one's foot, for example. Or looking across the street at the address you're searching for, instead of at your feet where the inevitable uneven piece of concrete lies in wait. That's what happened today.

Accuracy of foot placement, that's real. Any age can experience a spill, but it's more startling at 75. Shaking.

And when the trip or tumble occurs, feeling foolish is intensified by silver hair. The embarrassment, the sense of everyone's rushing to help the, um, elderly person. So uncool.

Therefore, I propose when faced with another article from an aging-gracefully fanatic, we rebel by kicking it down the road—this aging thing—like 10-year-olds chasing an empty can.

Old age lurches along; there's very little grace to it.

Tunes

My life does have a curious soundtrack, no matter what number the last birthday displays. Tunes are popped in for moments directly, it seems, by my unconscious, so that I've learned to say, "Really. Let's trace this back…why on Earth have I awakened with *I Can't Help Falling in Love with You* spooling through my brain?"

"You're so charming," I further complement her—my unconscious—to be sure she never feels left out. One cannot be too careful about such things.

Paris Metro tunnels are full of music. But, like we instructed our children when they wanted to toss francs into every musician's hat, I only give to the ones that practice.

A clarinetist who I'm sure held a chair in the Warsaw Symphony before emigrating, now sells his haunting classical melodies when I'm headed to the Cathedral. I can count on his presence to give my Sunday morning just the right send-off.

And I buy every CD he sells.

Before I know it, his offerings will no doubt be part of my personal soundtrack.

forty-four

Allez

On a warm, sunny morning in October as I emerged from the great iron gate across my cobblestones—often opened later on Sunday—a bunch of musicians that included a trombone and coronet were setting up at the Metro stairs: poised, ready to begin.

Since I was in a hurry to hear them, I lifted my arms as if in direction and with my gesture, their leader yelled, *ALLEZ*. And GO, they did.

Dancing in the sunshine, what a way to begin a day!

Part of me wanted to stay but after a considerable delay, I pulled out my euros, tossed them in the hat and took a CD along, instead. And kept dancing all the way through the Metro tunnels to the train.

It's Sunday. I know where I'm going.

forty-five
Wednesday = Mercredi

There is music in the Paris Metro, yes; music on the streets—especially on weekends—and in cafés, but the most exciting of all is upstairs at the warm, fragrant *creperie* two boulevards away from me on the Bastille roundabout, Boulevard Henri IV.

A flyer announced *le jazz* out on the sidewalk tables as I waft by one day. I return on Wednesday night at 21:00 when musicians begin to gather.

Emily leads the group, a willowy flautist, slim jeans and tall boots expressing her body and the flute giving voice to her soul. My beer is the only price of admission.

Sometimes various guitars join in; always a standing bass. My favorite, the piano, adds its very own particular percussion. When the room becomes packed with visiting musicians, Emily waves her delight, calling out *jam session*, inviting them to join in the music pronouncing it, *jam sessi-own*.

When Julie visited me on Cour Damoye, she, too, reveled in Mercredi at the creperie. After that when we found ourselves on a crowded Metro train she'd say with a grin, "Jam sessi-own..."

My Paris Wednesday night prayer meeting, and yes, it is divine.

forty-six

Bridges

We talk about transitions all the time: in ages, stages for toddlers or teens and right up through midlife into old age. But when we talk about *old age* we usually speak of other people; rarely of one's self.

Easier to joke, denigrate, shrug and privately despair the aging process, but when a new prescription—I once had a gerontologist who loaded me with six within two months—shows up, one may feel the aging process more keenly.

Sometimes I invite myself in for tea—or it might require something stronger—and I say, "Self, let's talk."

Facing a current lurch in the aging process doesn't mean giving up. It only means there's another possibility to consider: like crossing the Pont Marie from the 4th arrondissement and finding that I'm on l'Îsle Saint-Louis where the ancient café I adore—Aux Anysetiers du Roy—is only a block away.

It's so different from the Jewish Quartier or the Yiddish *Pletzl*—*little place*—on the other side in Le Marais. Here there's a different menu to explore.

I love the bridges of Paris. I love my life at every age.

 Audrey Ward

Centuries

La Brasserie de l'Île Saint-Louis is a landmark I pass so frequently, crossing to the Left Bank and back, that it could become commonplace. It never does. Her red awnings and rarified position of being in the middle of the Seine; looking into the gardens of Notre Dame as well as basking in the reflected lights from the water and sky, cause me to pause—if only for a few seconds—every time I pass.

Already well into a second century, she makes aging look glamorous with her terrace and interior overflowing in beautiful people day and night. And charming service? You have never experienced more lavish attention or praise. Even flirtation. It makes one feel more alive to be there.

Her owners, it is said, arrived shortly after France lost the Alsace-Lorraine to the Prussians in 1870. Many *restaurateurs* fled to Paris.

Perhaps it's the short story by Alphonse Daudet that I recall on the rare afternoon that I'm passing by early enough and find an open table: *The Last Lesson* is about a classroom in the Alsace-Lorraine on the final experience of French being spoken and taught.

I haven't read it for over 35 years; we found it in a book at a small hotel in Italy while traveling with our two youngest, Julie and Sam. We were living in the South of France at the time: they were 10 and eight, and we were keenly aware of being without our own language surrounding us everywhere we went.

Is this the real lesson of the warm red awnings and beautiful food that invite me into La Brasserie?

So many distant threads of time and place weave together the beauty of our reveries.

forty-eight

Sounds

Awaking in Paris makes me smile: rain against the windows or far-away city sounds whisper again where I am.

Then there's the room along the river on l'Îsle Saint-Louis, awaking to the crisp echo of horses' hooves. I jumped up and looked out to see four black horses ridden by dark blue-suited security officers along the quay.

The beauty arrested my eyes, first, as they passed beneath the fall gold of the plain trees. I wanted to replicate it, but I didn't want to take my eyes away even for a second to find my phone for the photograph.

And besides, it's like the poet said when finding a bird at evening singing in the woods. He couldn't take home the trees and the sky, the bird "sang to my ear, they sang to my eye."

Capturing a moment must sometimes simply rest in the heart.

forty-nine

Eternally

Paris is immediate. She demands attention from every sensory perception, especially if one's sight or sounds or tastes have been limited.

One short walk during market day—Tuesday—on the Boulevard Richard Lenoir, reveals the temporary stands, colorful, fragrant, and looking reasonably in order while out back of them, gnarled toughened hands hoist crates from the back of vans or wired-together trucks in from the country.

That, alone, provides adventure. But when I write sentiments such as:

> *I love my life*
> *all over again*
> *today…*

That rush of feeling is like an avalanche: sitting on a Parisian curb in a leafy glen on a balmy October afternoon listening to a coronet player with dulcet tones backing up a Sinatra cover, "The Best Is Yet to Come." All I could think of as I reveled in the moment was of my late, beloved, Bob Ward, whose name I still share. He would have relished everything about it.

Bob adored France; loved the language, but never spent a lot of time in Paris. Somehow, he seemed to believe he didn't deserve such pleasures and instead, crimped his life into smaller spaces. But through our travels together, he imparted a thirst for being here; for being present to grandeur and beauty wherever I can find it.

For this generous gift, I thank him eternally.

75

fifty

Pique-nique

One warm, Sunday night in October, feeling restless and unready to close down, stay in, I walked up Boulevard Henri IV to the Seine.

A surprise awaited me: as I leaned against the balustrade of the bridge, gazing below—about 21:00, 9:00 PM by my reckoning—I saw men, women, and children spreading blankets along the river's well-lit lawns for a *pique-nique*. Baguettes aplenty, cheeses and fruit or sandwiches made of baguettes plus bottles of wine were strewn everywhere among the people enjoying themselves in the friendly dark.

It was as if the sun was bright overhead and Monday morning, far away. How delicious was this freedom of turning the day upside-down.

The gate to Cour Damoye was shut when I returned, of course. Then I had the enchanting experience of *being home* by using my key to gain entry, leaning into the massive power of the iron closure.

Smiling all the while; ever after, too, remembering a picnic along the river banks on a Paris night.

 Audrey Ward

fifty-one

Shakespeare

As you walk up the half-painted, worn down stairs inside this disheveled book shop, each one comes nearer to finishing the sentence:

> *I wish I could*
> *show you when*
> *you are lonely or*
> *in darkness*
> *the astonishing*
> *light of your*
> *own being*
>
> – Haviz

At the room to the right, this night, a young Asian girl sits in a once overstuffed chair, legs tucked up under her plaid skirt, reading, while a calico cat sleeps on her lap. Across the unvarnished wood plank floor, a man sings, his voice dipping often to a whisper, strumming his Fender guitar.

Outside, fall is loitering in the air, leaves whispering the news as they wend their circular way to the sidewalk or the river; maybe to the roadway that hums with evening traffic. Flashing lights aid blue-uniformed men and women—whistles between their lips—in directing mostly little cars that situate themselves like a bumper-car carnival-ride at the intersection.

In this sprawling book shop, Shakespeare & Company, I read love poems as the singer sings, *Love is just a four-letter word*. And I wonder.

The bench outside the front door that stares across the Seine at Notre Dame, announces in somewhat crude, carved letters:

> *Open Door Open Books*
> *Open Mind Open Heart*

Kir

My idyllic memory of a perfect glass of white wine powered by a few drops of Crème de Cassis—Kir—is fixed in the countryside along the Loire River. Bob and I were out strolling one chilly, overcast Sunday afternoon near our *auberge*, Le Duc d'Anjou, and stopped into an ancient tavern for a drink.

Perhaps the white wine that was open that day—which is what one is supposed to use, "any leftover white wine"—was an exquisite dry burgundy. I don't know. But in all the years since that day in 1976, I had never had another that compared.

Not until Chez Julien in the Parisian neighborhood of St Paul Village. There was an event I was supposed to attend at the Cathedral that evening, but here I was, late afternoon, dawdling at a sidewalk table while gazing into the spectacular light gracing the river before me and lighting Our Lady, Notre Dame, in the distance.

As I reveled in the scene, three ladies of the night assembled on the corner across from the café: each one dressed to attract her own kind of customer one might imagine. A tall dashing young thing with deep chocolate-hued skin was in chic flats, lavender leather skirt skimming her thighs, and a brilliant pink beret tipped over her forehead, carrying a giant tote bag somewhat matching the beret. Another caramel-colored young one wore black head to toe. The third, tall, lithe, pale, in blue jeans, t-shirt and white Keds.

The Kir was exactly as I recalled our drink that afternoon along the Loire. In fact, I so enjoyed it, I had a second glass—usually a mistake, I find—yet it was, still, every bit as exquisite as the first.

Now, I wonder if it was the scene, the fascination of observing the young women, or the Kir that prolonged my stay.

Audrey Ward

Antitheist

When I encountered an atheist—or *anti-theist* as Richard Dawkins calls himself—one evening in the pub near my Paris apartment, I wasn't sure how to handle it for a change. Ordinarily, I say, "Oh yeah? What God is it you don't believe in?" There's a good chance that I don't believe in that God, either.

But this normally chatty, kind man went stone silent when my profession was mentioned. I knew he had heard of it already because another patron told him, so I intentionally lobbed it into our conversation which was instantly stopped. Dead stop.

Since I am a regular in this fine establishment—one might call it my "local"—I didn't press. And afterward, I considered whether to be more direct. I have to confess, this is a reaction I don't ever remember encountering.

People may be terribly injured at formative ages through the church, religion, priests, or clergy; plus, maybe parents who insist on a weekly practice. I take this seriously because in assessing my life with the help of professional listeners, it is clear that this is true of me.

As well intentioned as my parents were, they relied on 18th century child rearing policies that were absurdly restrictive. And, unfortunately, often considered "godly."

One theory was that the spirit of the child must be broken: the antithesis of anything spiritual, these methods are coercive and damaging.

When I was divorced, my mother tearfully confessed that she was sure my separation was happening because she had personally failed to break my spirit. Recognizing her distress, I only said,

"Mother, I am terribly sorry you're sad, but I am forever grateful that you failed."

In the end, I said nothing to my new friend in Paris. Our injuries belong to us as much as our inborn traits. The difference is, a hurt can heal, and if that is the case, healing will be up to him. Or not.

Biscuits

My first experience of the Adult Forum—an early Sunday educational gathering at the Cathedral—was titled, *The Celluloid Jesus*, tracing film images that went much further back than any of us in the room had guessed. I was hooked.

Afterward I asked Bill Tompson, the leader, for a quote he used by W. H. Auden. He proffered a corner of his notes for me to scribble my email address, promising to send it later that day.

In return for the quote that evening, I wrote that I appreciated the rare depth of this class, citing my experience as a pastor.

A few minutes later, I received another email, thanking me and then saying straightaway that he had taken the liberty of Googling me. What a surprise for both of us that we have a beloved mentor in common.

Dr. Fred Craddock was Bill's professor of New Testament when he was an undergraduate at Emory in Atlanta. He relayed to me phrases remembered from those days that still serve as guide and wisdom. Now, Tompson has a Doctorate from Oxford and an international position in Paris having to do with Russian language and diplomacy.

Seeing that Fred had insisted on my writing a book—*Hidden Biscuits, Tales of Deep South Revivals Told by Heart*—about my early life as an itinerant evangelist's daughter in the Deep South, Bill was even more curious. Dr. Craddock wrote the Forward for my memoir published in 2015.

Right away, he insisted that the Cathedral host me as a leader of the Forum with the book *Hidden Biscuits*. My parents would have been stunned to know that the story of their humble travels among their treasured, often illiterate Appalachian people was told and well received by a standing-room-only audience at The American Cathedral in Paris.

What a day that was for all of us, including my mother, father and older sister, Althea. They were with me for every moment.

Awe

It was that particular morning when, as we awaited the procession that begins the liturgy in the aisle of the Cathedral—the choir singing, liturgists robed, thrusting high the cross—that I observed a small boy of about two or three standing in the pew just ahead of me.

He was with his grandparents, one on either side, and he faced the door where the procession had formed, person by person. The rector, Dean Lucinda Laird is last in line, resplendent in brocade and embroidered garments.

As he watched, the child's eyes grew larger, then larger still; his mouth fell open, and when the first choral sounds were emitted and the entire assemblage began to move, he said with holy awe drawn out, beginning in a whisper, "Wowwwww…"

And that, I thought, *is why it matters to bring small children into the sanctuary.*

fifty-six

Noise

We were walking along the River Seine a block from the elementary school on Île Saint Louis, when their children burst out of the doors for *déjeuner* at mid-day. The beautiful noise; music of their laughter, prompted Wendy to say, "Children sound different here—different from kids in the U.S."

How so?

Since Wendy teaches a kindergarten class—24 children a day crowding through her life—I consider her an expert witness.

"There's an easy pace to their hilarity." She paused, then, "It seems full of vigor. I've observed them in the parks, too—making up teams to play kick ball or a game that's like 'red rover'—or singing together. Impromptu!"

She found this both startling and encouraging for children of the world. All colors and ages joining in the games together.

"What does it mean when you say 'easy pace?'" I pressed.

"Not so intense…competitive. That's what I seem to be hearing: *more fun than competition.*"

Her words make me wonder what we are teaching our children as we dash out the door, checking our cell phones on the run.

 Audrey Ward

Route 69

Parisians do value children. I noticed this while taking the bus whose route curls through elegant streets, arriving, finally at the Champ du Mar (Tour Eiffel).

A grandmother boards with her elementary school aged grandson, bringing him home from the classes of the day. As we go, she is quizzing him all along the route about the buildings, their purpose, and various statues poised at the edge of a park.

This transmission of culture by oral tradition is a priceless gift to the child. And, perhaps, you have already guessed: she didn't glance at a cell phone even one time.

But she did smile at me and wink, as if to say, "Isn't this boy a wonder?"

And so are you, I thought to myself.

Rambling

Often in my travels, as I pause on a park bench in the Tuileries, have a beer at an Austrian pub, or lunch in an Italian café gazing out over Lake Como; perhaps sipping a Swiss white wine, elixir divine; stealing a spoon full of ice cream from Will's dish in Prague, this phrase occurs to me: *What would I miss most if I was not here?*

Or, perhaps, meeting Lauren at the Hotel d'Aubusson, my favorite Left Bank hang out. We order martinis since she's over 21 and besides, my guy here knows how I like them, and we reminisce about the last place we met far from home, coming up out of the subway in the Village, New York, headed to dinner at the Minetta Tavern. *What would I miss most if I was not here?*

This phrase is scribbled all through my tiny blue notebook tucked in a pocket. Now, I'm thinking it's a worthy question to ask myself every day.

Those words could add a layer of appreciation for every minute of my life. For every breath.

No matter whether I'm at an exotic address or at my kitchen table enjoying warm oatmeal, life is a treasure. Even in the midst of deep concerns for family or friends after murmuring their names as I light a candle, I return to the great goodness I am granted each new morning.

Since we seldom have a choice in the outcome, why not bless the day *as is*.

Shine

> Seeing the crimson cyclamen
> on the kitchen counter
> after her refreshment,
> I kiss her, saying,
> "Good morning." Even though
>
> it's somber outside
> in this early hour, still,
> there's well enough time
> to shine: It's a Paris morning,
> and that means that I shine.

After my coffee and some tidbit from the *boulangerie* I brought home last night for my *petit déjeuner* this morning, I'm down the stairs and tapping along the wet cobblestones in the drizzle. Maybe the giant iron gate isn't yet open, so I give my full force to her swinging wide.

How I love the effort, opening into the buzz of people headed to the Metro as I am, or to one of the cafes that flank both sides of the gate. Maybe one of the buses; there are five lines that come to this radius of corners.

It's morning in Paris, so wherever I'm going what does it matter?

Train Bleu Gare de Lyon

Now, coming and going, one
seldom looks up
to notice the elegance
at the top of the stairs.
Instead, eyes scan
Departures, awaiting a *voie numero*
for her own private destination,
or, if perchance an obnoxious
fellow traveler's case rolls
over one's delicate toes,
then loud and clear swear words
swipe across Departures
and scowls erase the
ease of bland flicking
through the overhead
screen. Once upon a time
it was better, this going and coming:
Grand billboards loudly clacked
information into place.
Then. That's it, *then,* yes,
Train Bleu was born
into a world not at all
automatic. One arrived early
for tea, café, or an aperitif
at the elegant room up the stairs.
Opulent, with murals of
destinations in the South of France;

Audrey Ward

named for the luxury train
that would take them there.

Painters sat by the sea
creating the form for the murals
foreseen. And here am I,
gold-crested cup in hand
reveling in the scenes they loved, too.
Remembering, just as they.

Sea

Sea in this context, refers to the Mediterranean that kisses the South of France with affection and—in some cases—notorious fun. When we lived five kilometers from Bandol our family adored Renecros, the sheltered, crescent beach a short walk from the village.

While the children played in the sand or peddled in a small boat along the shore, Bob and I would have an elegant three-course lunch. That included a carafe of rosé at the café—watching the kids all the while—'neath our umbrella on the terrace.

The waters are not only clear, sparkling blue—just like the murals at Train Bleu—they are placid on sun-filled days of spring and early summer. We decided we would leave as soon as the tourists from northern Europe descended in July. It was an excellent plan.

Meantime, strolling on the sand or taking a cruise along the cliffs—*les calanques*—from Bandol to Cassis or even as far as Marseilles (about 35 kilometers by car), the white sculptures nature has arranged through the centuries demand astonishment, even reverence.

Seeing depictions in vivid, golden hued-pastels on the walls of Train Bleu reminds me: the wonders of this world are worth pursuing.

Laughter

On a rainy day along the Boulevard Beaumarchais, a tea room charmed me into edging my way through her merry crowd, fabrics of roses and polka dots draped about. Tables with Plexiglas tops display old jewelry some might call "junk," but here appears perfectly charming.

Wedged into a corner, I order a rose-scented brew. The girls next door whisper and laugh their musical French. Once again, I deplore my capacity to eavesdrop adequately in this language, but the laughter is delicious.

And so, in the midst of a dripping grey day, my spirits become as rosy as their chatter while they share the secrets of friendship. I sip my *thé noir avec des roses* and smile.

Happiness translates beauty well into every language; I can always eavesdrop on this, however it's expressed in words.

She

Dark waters send
long boats
with their cargo
of curious tourists
swiftly along
the Seine. Some
carriers tacky
with neon lights;
others sleek,
mysterious
as midnight
(the same
can be said
of the travelers).

Our lady, the river
tells none
of her secrets
to the wind
or the trees
along the Quai,
and she
always keeps
the tales
that strangers tell
her in their travels
strictly to herself.

Audrey Ward

She's especially
silent in bright lights:
No one whispers there.

Vignette

Four mounted policemen just trotted by under the window on l'Îsle Saint-Louis. I didn't know they existed in Paris. They do, blue uniforms brilliant with black trim; perfect posture on midnight steeds of equally impressive form.

Marching in time with the wind, it seems.

And a red-headed lass walks along just beside them toward Boulevard Henri IV, her long unruly hair streaming with the breeze.

Curious: Are they protection for her, or is she distraction for them?

Yes.

Brigade Fluviale

Blue lights flashing, the Brigade Fluviale, Paris's river police force, rush to the scene: watching them pass under a bridge at top speed is breathtaking. And one immediately thinks, where to! What's happening.

They are an elite group that patrol about 370 miles of waterways in and around Paris. Thousands of tourist boats load and unload passengers; commercial freight vehicles travel goods up and down. The lifesaving skills of the River Brigade are as necessary as their peace-keeping capacity.

In the midnight hours, they may be called on for a would-be suicide, rescuing someone from the turbulent waters. Tides are unpredictable, and at some places, it seems that the currents are traveling against each other.

And, of course, there are the times when by accident or by purpose, they must take a body from the waters. This is not a job for the faint of heart.

To be a guardian, one must be under the age of 40; an excellent swimmer and experienced in boating. Even so, the training is arduous, and the capacity of the guardian cannot be overestimated.

So much of the life in this city depends upon them; their own lives depend on them as well.

Meeting

Le Grand Colbert

Just up a rise from the back walls of Le Grand Palais with her sweeping, walled courtyard, a warren of little streets in the theater district harbor fine aromas; a golden indoor shopping mall and Le Grand Colbert.

You probably remember it, if at all, from the Nancy Meyers' film *Something's Gotta Give*, where former lovers, Diane Keaton as playwright Erica Barry, and Jack Nicholson as Harry Sanborn, reunite on her birthday. Her current man, Keanu Reeves (Julian Mercer) is her date, but of course this small detail fails to hinder the course of true love.

Meeting friends for a meal—whether lunch or dinner—is enchanting at this restaurant, I must confess. Not just a tourist trap in my estimation, but brimming with brio and servers pleased to be there, bringing on fine food.

When one walks into Le Grand Colbert a rush of warmth welcomes from tall, sweeping branches of trees strung with sparkle; ancient statues peer over you, and mirrors reflect the brilliance. Simoné and Fiona were there to meet me on their way from Great Britain to Rome for a visit to his family. He and I studied together at Oxford, but this was my first introduction to his companion.

It's the laughter and thumbing through memories in a graceful setting that is most treasured. I've visited Simoné and his grandmother, Clelia, in Venice at her place on Lido Isle—after he had spent a couple of weeks at my house in the Napa Valley—and now, we meet in-between.

　　　Audrey Ward

International friends may turn up anywhere in the world. Maybe next time it will be, well, who knows?

Words

Some phrases in French have no match in our language. When we lived there, they all said we spoke *American*.

Like, *Je suis dépitée* is, *I am mad and sad*. Wish we had a word like that: mad and sad? Really. While the language itself has fewer words than ours does, their expressions and way of using text seem unusually creative.

Je suis tombée des nues, says one is *flabbergasted*, but means, literally, *I fell from the clouds*. Isn't that how flabbergasted feels? Oh, and *faire du léche-vitrine*, meaning in American *to lick the glass*, is the French phrase for *window shopping*.

Such encounters with their language also cause me to harbor a creeping suspicion that no matter how long I study French and struggle along, there may never be a sense of thorough understanding.

When we inhabited the South of France with our two younger children—eight and 10 at the time—our friend Patrick said to me, shrugging, "If you come to a word or phrase that you don't know, just throw in something like *carrot* or *cabbage*. No one will know the difference." Nevertheless, I faithfully carried around a small notebook to record phrases I could not decipher when they were quickly said.

One evening as we were sipping aperitifs at *chez amis*, someone referred to the Scotch as being so smooth that it was *le bébé Jesus qui glisse dans un pantalon de velours*. Of course his words slipped by so fast I had to say, "Wait, wait! What was that?"

This potion was, he patiently explained, so smooth that it was like, *little baby Jesus sliding down in velvet pants*.

      Audrey Ward

Picking myself up after having fallen from the clouds laughing, I agreed.

Dazzling

Winter sunshine dims early in the evening, but the sky along the Seine just at the Pont Saint Louis at the back of Notre Dame, gathers every fragment for its use in dazzling anyone fortunate to be there.

Here I am.

The mulled wine is more expensive at Berthillon, of course, with her commanding view of river skyline and music wafting over from performers on the bridge, but what a sweet place to revel in the scene.

My down coat snugs around me, reaching to my boot tops; more than one scarf wraps my head and shoulders warm as I sip hot spiced wine in the glowing air. Really: there's a pink cast to the particulate matter in the atmosphere settling around us.

Photos I take of the café across the way—La Brasserie de l'Îsle Saint-Louis—proves the colors that are vivid in the sky. How can one be other than enchanted?

Tonight, I do not mind that I'm not capable of eavesdropping in French. Silence serves me well.

Hospitality

Even in my tiny Cour Damoye kitchen, I love to cook. Especially for a guest, and gathering ingredients for an evening's get together is never more pleasurable than in Paris.

The truth is that in California or any place else, I feel the same. But fresh baguette or vegetables are gorgeous in a marché setting as the farmer's wife weighs them and writes the amount in pencil on her tablet for me to see.

When the time arrives, lighting the candle and pouring the wine is the opening moment of welcome. Ahhh…as far as I'm concerned, the persons I invite have fulfilled all "duty" when they walk in and enjoy the evening with me.

And yet, while that is true, I also wonder that so few people have a clue about being hospitable.

Clergy, I confess, are some of the worst. In the church, we are charged with being people of hospitality; are we so busy doing *God's work* we often fail to do that which is beautifully human?

Some of my seminary friends suggested my tombstone would one day read: *She Loved Lunch*. Personally, I'm happy to go with that.

Larkin

Philip Larkin wrote a poem named *Church Going* that has followed me everywhere in Europe. My friend John Sam first quoted lines to me. After that, when I wrote it out and ardently attempted to memorize the piece, Larkin's words began to stalk me. In a good way.

The day I take the train to Chartre, I savor the phrases and their meaning as I gaze at the golden fields and villages—an occasional steeple which always gives grace to a landscape—as we pass.

I suspect that I'm arrested with the power of these verses since there's so much talk in this era, if the subject is considered at all, about the ineffective *so-what* of church going. *Who needs it except morons and weaklings?* seems to be the general idea.

William Sloane Coffin, late pastor of the Riverside Church in New York, had a ready answer for those who said that religion was a crutch, "And who says you don't limp?"

But Larkin ends his meditation with the idea that this hallowed place, even when abandoned by time and people, still gives us a space where it is possible to grow wise. There. That's it.

Envy

A pair of swans
whom I first saw
in the evening
while I strolled
along the Seine
on *l'Île Saint-Louie,*
floated by my window
early today.

Last night, they were sleeping
tucked in, heads under wings,
so close to each other, a few
feathers were touching
side by side at river's edge.

What companionable sounds
do swans make, I wonder.
And the list for this day:
ports most likely to find
le petite déjeuner. Maybe.

Being together, though,
this is the main event.

Heard

And the preacher says before she begins—at the Cathedral in Paris— *Between the words spoken and the words heard may the spirit of God be present.*

A message of trust, then, encourages the hearer before a single word of her prepared remarks land. The speaker's words come in for a landing. Or not. Sometimes they drift around and, I've suspected, disappear like fine mist with the sun's emergence.

My focus in preparation is upon what I'm learning that can make a difference for my own self because I know if I can't hear it for myself, no one else will, either.

It's a tricky business, this public speaking. One never knows who is in the audience.

When I was particularly exercised about a matter of injustice while sending my words on their way one Sunday, a man up front whom I'd never seen before turned very solemn. At the door, he took my hand and, holding it softly said in a whisper, "I was raised in a *pacifist* home."

I wasn't sure if perhaps I had frightened him with my vehemence? It seemed that I had. My words came down in his warning zone, *high danger alert.*

So, *Between the words spoken and words heard...* Come to think of it, words may need a shock absorber no matter where they're said.

Generations

Threading the years through miles, creating new memories while reveling in the long-ago, surprised my seventy-fifth year with enough delight to flood my cup to the brim and roll right over. And still, there were bonuses.

First, daughter Julie arrived from California late one rainy October night, calling me to open the gate. I was down three flights of steps and out the door before she could take another breath.

My Parisian buddy, Kris, brought in a photographer for some shots of us along my lane: One of them graces the back of this book.

After that, late November, twenty-one year old Lauren, Tamara's—my older daughter--and Dan's young one flew into town, a Texas tornado.

They insisted on excursions I would probably not have indulged in by myself. Julie had reservations for a dinner cruise, an extra gift from Tom who was tending their three offspring at home. One should not miss swiftly gliding under Paris bridges through the shadows. At evening's end as our beloved Lady of Liberty whose twin stands in New York's harbor, comes into view, we see the Tour Eiffel as her companion. Breathtaking.

Maybe growing old also means that one is so full of beauty that when scenes such as this appear, tears of gratitude readily spill. Wonder. At the privilege of being here, now, a witness with someone we love.

Flashing away from the Gard du Nord on the Eurostar, French countryside rushing past our window, then arriving in St Pancras International, Kings Cross, London, was the rousing finish for Julie's visit. Plus a weekend at a Kensington Hotel with a lot of revelry on tap.

Lauren and I took the Eurostar like a boomerang in one long day. By then sparkling angels stretched over intersections outside Liberty of London—by far, my favorite department store—for the Christmas Season.

And now these indelible memories hold us close just as we hold each other.

Audrey Ward

News

A lot of the news that's taken over American channels in the Twenty-First Century is more akin to gossip than headline-deserving information. But even those tidbits are harder to come by if I'm out of my own language loop.

When our family was living in Provence in 1980 there was no wifi of course, so there was scant information from America and no good gossip at all. We almost missed what would now be a huge hit on the 24-hour news cycle: California's Governor Jerry Brown dating rock star Linda Ronstadt.

We were enlightened by our friend Jim's page of three-dot journalism sent by snail mail from home. None of it mean or unkind, just bits of celebrity sightings since he knew the grapevine didn't reach all the way to the South of France.

Linda did have such wonderful fun with Jerry during that era. And from what I hear, though they haven't dated for decades, they're still friends. Some news stays good, after all.

Seventy-five

Heavenly

Some places warm you with memories even as you walk by: L'Ange is one of those tiny bistros that beckon because the aroma, anticipation and enjoyment of their food and wine are always with you.

Plus, Christopher invites you: he who tends incoming guests as well as those already seated.

My last dinner there was with Stephanie, a young jazz singer who not only introduced me to her buddies from London, Lou and Madie, but to a fabulous lipstick named Ruby Woo. And then Lou, who's an artist at this sort of thing taught me how to apply it correctly. See how certain places string your pearls together in a dazzling array of remembrance?

There's a lamb dish on the menu I'm confident I will never be capable of creating myself. It is slow-cooked for seven hours and yet the flavor and texture are only enhanced. I've looked everywhere for a recipe that imitates this with no success.

L'Ange is only one of many small offerings along the streets of this city. It would be foolish as well as impossible to attempt numbering them.

I've surrendered: there are experiences in taste, visions, vistas and quality of light that can only be achieved here. My hunch is that this is what writers have in mind when they extol the wonders of a heavenly city prepared for certain saints as a reward for a well-lived earthly life.

Paris is that reward here and now.

When I planned to spend these two months here, I imagined this would be a farewell tour. But now I don't think so. Paris is being woven into my life; she belongs as part of my personal tapestry.

                    Audrey Ward